EUREKA!
I've discovered
Electricity

Britt Norlander

mc Marshall Cavendish
Benchmark
New York

Marshall Cavendish Benchmark
99 White Plains Road
Tarrytown, NY 10591
www.marshallcavendish.us

All Internet addresses were available and accurate when this book went to press.

Library of Congress Cataloging-in-Publication Data
Norlander, Britt.
I've discovered electricity! / by Britt Norlander.
p. cm. -- (Eureka!)
Includes bibliographical references and index.
ISBN 978-0-7614-3195-4
1. Electricity--Juvenile literature. 2. Discoveries in science--Juvenile literature. 3. Scientists--
Juvenile literature. 4. Inventions--Juvenile literature. I. Title.
QC527.2.N668 2009
537--dc22
2008014834

The photographs in this book are used by permission and through the courtesy of:
Cover: Q2A Media Art Bank
Half Title : Peter Menzel/SPL/ Photolibrary
Tischenko Irina/Shutterstock: P4; Peter Menzel/SPL/Photolibrary: P7 tl;
Alexkhrom/Dreamstime.com: P7b; Liviufaur/ Dreamstime.com: P11; Italian School,
(19th century)/Visual Arts Library (London)/Alamy: P12; Jarek Szymanski/istockphoto: P15tr;
Johnson Space Center/NASA: P15b; Shutterstock: P19 All; Edison, Thomas Alva
(1847-1931)/Visual Arts Library (London)/ Alamy: P20; Martinyu/Dreamstime.com: P23tr;
Shapiso/Shutterstock: P23tl; Mrspants/Dreamstime.com: P23bl;
Milos Luzanin/Shutterstock: P23br; Pavol Kmeto/Shutterstock: P27
Illustrations: Q2A Media Art Bank

Created by Q2AMedia
Creative Director: Simmi Sikka
Series Editor: Jessica Cohn
Art Director: Sudakshina Basu
Designer: Dibakar Acharjee
Illustrators: Amit Tayal, Aadil Ahmed, Rishi Bhardwaj,
Kusum Kala, Pooja Shukla and Sanyogita Lal
Photo research: Sejal Sehgal
Senior Project Manager: Ravneet Kaur
Project Manager: Shekhar Kapur

Printed in Malaysia

Contents

Opposites Attract

Electricity powers your television and helps your iPod play your favorite songs. This power actually comes from **atoms**. Inside atoms are tiny **particles**. Electrical energy comes from tiny particles called **electrons**. They zip around inside the atoms that make up every object and living thing—including you!

Sometimes, electrons jump from one atom to another. As electrons move between two objects, they cause those objects to build up an electrical charge. That is called **static electricity**.

If you've ever had one of your socks stick to a sweatshirt when they came out of the dryer, you've seen static electricity. While your clothes tumbled around in the dryer, electrons moved between the sock and the sweatshirt. That caused one of them to build a positive charge. It caused the other to gain a negative charge. Objects with opposite charges are attracted to each other.

Have you ever felt a shock when you touched a doorknob after walking across a carpet? That's static electricity, too! The shock was caused by electrons jumping from you to the doorknob.

Earth's magnetic field moves the needle.

Meet William Gilbert

William Gilbert (1544–1603) was the first person to use the term *electric*. Gilbert was trained as a doctor. He even served as the physician to Queen Elizabeth I of England. Yet Gilbert also did many experiments on the properties of static electricity and **magnetism**. In 1600, he published a book called *De Magnete*, which means "On the Magnet" in Latin. The book described everything that was known about electricity and magnetism at that time. Gilbert was the first person to explain how a magnetic **compass** works. He discovered that Earth is like a giant magnet. The magnetic forces of Earth move the needle of the compass.

Create Static Electricity

You Will Need:

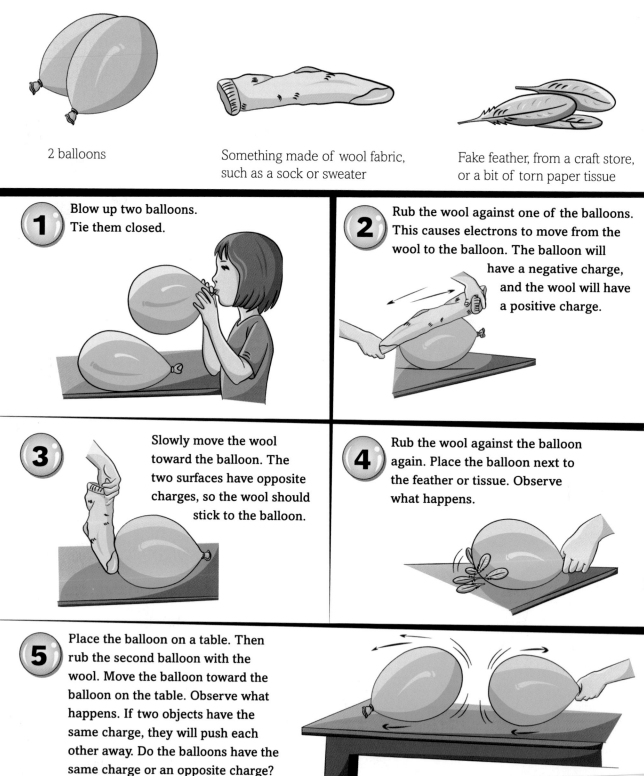

2 balloons

Something made of wool fabric, such as a sock or sweater

Fake feather, from a craft store, or a bit of torn paper tissue

1 Blow up two balloons. Tie them closed.

2 Rub the wool against one of the balloons. This causes electrons to move from the wool to the balloon. The balloon will have a negative charge, and the wool will have a positive charge.

3 Slowly move the wool toward the balloon. The two surfaces have opposite charges, so the wool should stick to the balloon.

4 Rub the wool against the balloon again. Place the balloon next to the feather or tissue. Observe what happens.

5 Place the balloon on a table. Then rub the second balloon with the wool. Move the balloon toward the balloon on the table. Observe what happens. If two objects have the same charge, they will push each other away. Do the balloons have the same charge or an opposite charge?

WHO WOULD HAVE THOUGHT?

People were experimenting with electricity well over two thousand years ago. Scientists in Ancient Greece rubbed fur and cloth against **amber.** That is a fluid from trees that has become a hard fossil. The ancient scientists discovered that the rubbed amber attracts objects such as feathers, though they didn't know why. Yet this attractive force is the result of static electricity. The word *electricity* comes from the Greek word for amber, *elektron*.

Lightning Strikes!

Benjamin Franklin became interested in electricity after seeing a **Leyden jar** in action. This special glass jar stores static electricity. When you touch it with a metal wire, a spark jumps in the jar. Franklin thought that spark looked a lot like lightning. He wondered: Is lightning caused by electricity? He designed an experiment to find out.

If he could tell you the story . . .

Meet Benjamin Franklin

Benjamin Franklin (1706–1790) was born into a big family in Boston, Massachusetts. Throughout his life, Franklin made many new scientific discoveries and inventions. Many of these inventions had to do with his daily life. When he was ten years old, he made the world's first swim fins. He made round wooden paddles that he strapped to his hands and feet. They helped him show off for his friends by swimming faster and farther than ever before.

As Franklin got older, his eyesight started to go bad. He needed glasses to see objects up close and different glasses to see things in the distance. Tired of always having to change his glasses, he invented **bifocals**. These glasses help people see clearly objects that are both near and far away.

WHAT A SHOCKING IDEA!

In 1752, I went to a field near Philadelphia during a thunderstorm.

I flew a kite that had a metal point on it and a metal key tied to its string.

During thunderstorms, charged particles build up in the clouds.

Some of those charged particles jumped onto the kite.

Do you know what happened when I reached a knuckle toward the metal key?

ZAP!—electrical charges gave me a shock!

Franklin's experiment proved that lightning was static electricity. Yet what he did was actually very dangerous. The next two scientists who tried the experiment were struck by very strong electrical charges and died.

Create a Little Lightning

You Will Need:

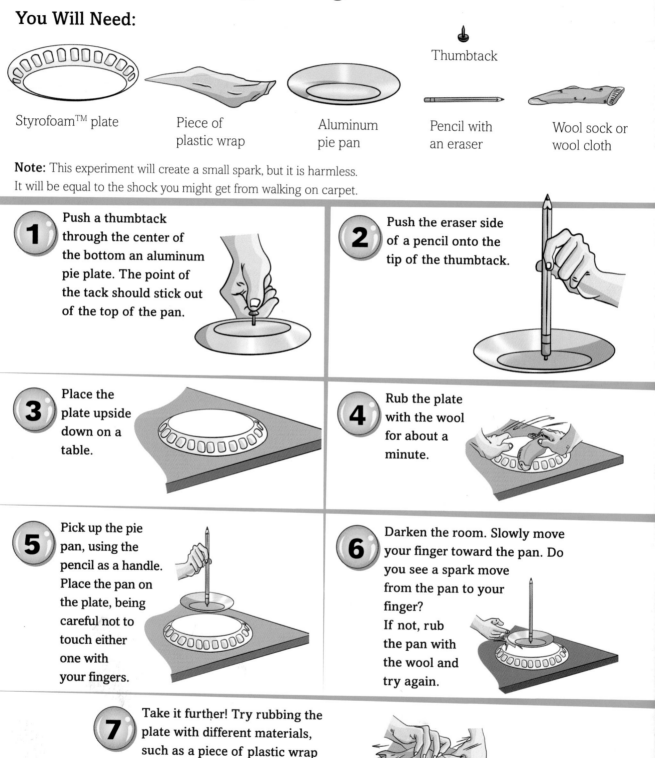

Styrofoam™ plate

Piece of plastic wrap

Aluminum pie pan

Thumbtack

Pencil with an eraser

Wool sock or wool cloth

Note: This experiment will create a small spark, but it is harmless. It will be equal to the shock you might get from walking on carpet.

1 Push a thumbtack through the center of the bottom an aluminum pie plate. The point of the tack should stick out of the top of the pan.

2 Push the eraser side of a pencil onto the tip of the thumbtack.

3 Place the plate upside down on a table.

4 Rub the plate with the wool for about a minute.

5 Pick up the pie pan, using the pencil as a handle. Place the pan on the plate, being careful not to touch either one with your fingers.

6 Darken the room. Slowly move your finger toward the pan. Do you see a spark move from the pan to your finger? If not, rub the pan with the wool and try again.

7 Take it further! Try rubbing the plate with different materials, such as a piece of plastic wrap or a nylon stocking. Which one produces the longest spark?

WHO WOULD HAVE THOUGHT?

Franklin went on to invent the **lightning rod**. That is a metal rod placed on top of a building. Electricity travels through metal easily. When lightning strikes near a building with a lightning rod, the electricity travels through the rod. That way it does not travel through the building.

Before lightning rods existed, many houses and buildings burned down when they were struck by lightning. The Empire State Building in New York City receives about one hundred lightning strikes a year. Luckily, the lightning bolts are drawn to lightning rods on top of the building.

Go with the Flow

For many years, scientists experimented with static electricity. They learned to create sparks of electricity. The first sparks they worked with did not last long. They wanted to find a way to create sparks that lasted longer, so that the sparks might be used to power things.

In 1800, Alessandro Volta (1745–1827) created the electric battery. It was the first item that could produce a flow of electricity that did not stop. His invention was called a **voltaic pile**.

Volta's battery was a stack of three types of small **disks**. He used **zinc** disks, **copper** disks, and disks made of a material like cardboard. The third type was soaked in a vinegar or salt solution. Volta connected a wire to the top and bottom of the pile. Electrons flowed from the copper disks to the zinc disks through the salt solution. That created an electric **current**—a flow of electrons.

In addition to the voltaic pile, Volta invented an **electrophorous**, an invention used to store an electric charge and deliver it to another object. Volta did a lot of wonderful things with electricity. The unit of electric force was named in his honor in 1881. A **volt** is a measure of the strength of a flowing charge.

We can control the energy flow.

Meet Luigi Galvani

Luigi Galvani (1737–1798) gave Volta the idea for the battery. Galvani, a doctor, was dissecting a dead frog to study its body. Suddenly the frog jumped! He had touched two different parts of the frog's body with two different metals. That caused the frog's tissues to make a sharp movement. Galvani thought he had discovered electricity in animals. When Volta heard the story, however, he thought it must have something to do with the metals Galvani was using. Volta started experimenting with different metals to come up with his battery.

Make a Battery

You Will Need:

Glass of water

1 teaspoon of salt

1 teaspoon of vinegar

Paper towels

Scissors

5 pennies
5 dimes

Voltmeter, from a hardware store (optional)

1 Pour water into a small glass until it is half full. Add a teaspoon of salt and a teaspoon of vinegar to the water. Mix well.

2 Cut nine 1-inch-by-1-inch pieces of paper towel.

3 Soak the paper towel squares in the salt and vinegar mixture.

4 Place a dime on a table. Cover it with a wet towel. Put a penny on that towel. Cover the penny with another towel. Repeat until the last penny is on top.

5 Wet the tips of your two index fingers. Then hold the pile of coins between your fingers. You should feel a little shock or tingle on your fingers. What you are feeling is a small—and safe—current of electricity.

6 If you have one, use a voltmeter to measure the electric current created by your battery. Touch the red (positive) wire from the voltmeter to the penny. Touch the black (negative) wire to the dime. What is the voltage?

WHO WOULD HAVE THOUGHT?

The batteries we use today are based on Volta's battery from 1800. They are used to power everything from tiny music players to the **International Space Station**. **Solar panels** on the space station **convert** the Sun's energy into electricity. That electricity is stored in batteries. The electricity is available for delivery even when the station is in darkness.

Magnets and Motors

Like many scientists during his time, Michael Faraday was interested in magnetism and electricity. He thought a lot about how they are connected. It was said that he carried a small rod of iron and a bit of wire in his pocket. Whenever he had a chance, he would experiment with them.

Eventually, he made an important discovery. He proved that when an electrical current flows, it creates a magnetic field. Magnets that work this way are called **electromagnets**.

Faraday invented the electric motor in 1821. He made the **dynamo** in 1831. A dynamo turns movement into electricity. The energy of movement is sometimes called **mechanical energy**. A motor does the opposite of what a dynamo does. It turns electricity into mechanical energy. A motor makes movement.

Meet Michael Faraday

Michael Faraday (1791–1867) was born in London, England. His father was a blacksmith. Faraday's family was so poor that as a boy, sometimes the only thing he had to eat for a whole week was a loaf of bread. His love of science grew after reading about electricity. He soon started doing science experiments of his own.

As an adult, Faraday wanted to pass on his love for science to children. He gave a series of talks called the Christmas Lectures at the Royal Institution of Great Britain, in London. The most famous of these was published in a book, *The History of the Candle*. It was all about candles and flames. The Christmas lectures are still held in his honor every year.

I DIDN'T MEAN TO SCARE YOU!

I realized that a wire carrying an electric current would swing around a magnet…but the electric current could also make the magnet move around it.

The movement is due to the electromagnetic forces from the wire and magnet pushing against each other.

When I move a magnet in and out of a coil of wire, an electric current flows through the wire. So magnetism can be used to make electric motors turn.

Push the magnet in and the current flows one way…

Push the magnet out and the current flows the other way.

17

MAKE YOUR OWN ELECTROMAGNET

You Will Need:

D-cell battery

Metal nail

Metal paper clips with no coating

Several feet of insulated wire

Note: Have an adult scrape the insulation off the ends of the copper wire.

1 Start about a foot from the wire's end. Wrap the wire tightly around a nail ten times.

2 Attach one end of the wire to each of the two **terminals** on the battery.

3 Touch the end of the nail to a paper clip. See how many clips are picked up by the magnetized nail.

4 Take the wire off the battery. Then loop the wire twenty times around the nail, in the same direction as before. Rehook it to the battery. Try again to pick up clips. The strength of the magnetic field should increase.

If your electromagnet doesn't work, try the following:

1 Check the wire connections to your battery.

2 Make more loops around the nail.

3 Try picking up smaller objects.

4 Try a different metal nail.

Note: You can also use a D cell battery if you tape the wire to the battery's top with electrical tape.

WHO WOULD HAVE THOUGHT?

Faraday's simple electric motor did not do much. Yet his invention led other people to use electricity to do other things. His dynamo idea is still being used. Dynamos are at work inside power plants. They provide electricity to homes and businesses.

That's Bright!

Thomas Edison knew that one of the greatest things that electricity could provide was electric light. Edison experimented to create a safe electric light bulb. He tried to make one that would last a long time.

He worked with three thousand different materials before 1879, when he found one that lasted for forty hours. His light bulb had a **filament** that heats up when an electric current runs through it. The filament becomes so hot that it begins to glow. How would he then power the bulbs in everyone's homes?

Edison opened the Pearl Street Central Power Station in New York City in 1882. His power station provided a flow of electricity. He made his power station produce a current in which electrons flowed in one direction. This was an important step in creating the systems that provide electricity to the public today.

We can eventually light buildings!

Meet Thomas Edison

Thomas Edison (1847–1931) was born in Ohio. As a young boy, he enjoyed reading and doing experiments in his basement. He struggled in school, however, perhaps because he was hard of hearing. Thomas went to school for only three months. After that, his mother home-schooled him.

Thomas started working as a paperboy at the age of twelve. He was hard-working and continued to do experiments every chance he got. He even went back to his laboratory to work on his wedding day. All of that hard work paid off. Thomas Edison created more than a thousand inventions during his lifetime.

Create an Electric Current

You Will Need:

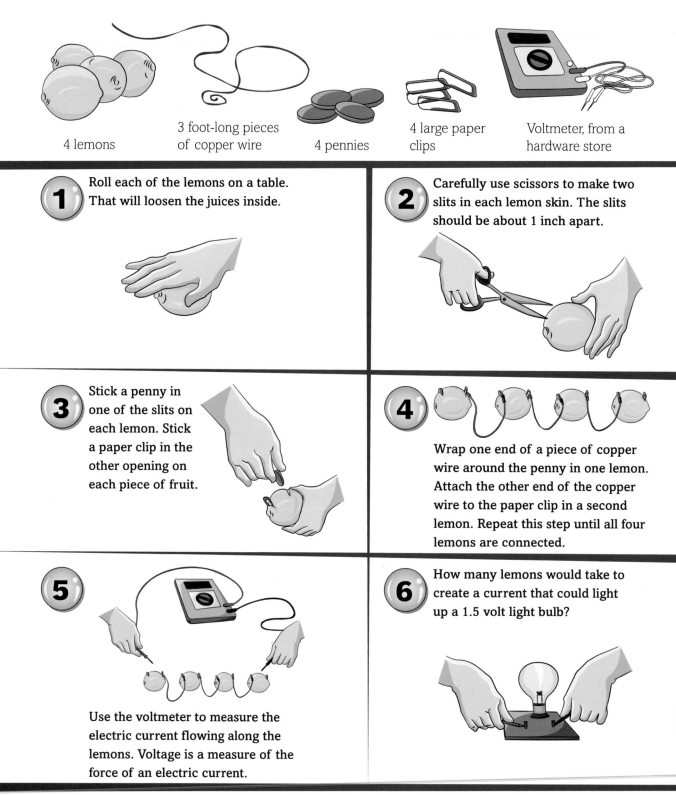

4 lemons

3 foot-long pieces of copper wire

4 pennies

4 large paper clips

Voltmeter, from a hardware store

1 Roll each of the lemons on a table. That will loosen the juices inside.

2 Carefully use scissors to make two slits in each lemon skin. The slits should be about 1 inch apart.

3 Stick a penny in one of the slits on each lemon. Stick a paper clip in the other opening on each piece of fruit.

4 Wrap one end of a piece of copper wire around the penny in one lemon. Attach the other end of the copper wire to the paper clip in a second lemon. Repeat this step until all four lemons are connected.

5 Use the voltmeter to measure the electric current flowing along the lemons. Voltage is a measure of the force of an electric current.

6 How many lemons would take to create a current that could light up a 1.5 volt light bulb?

WHO WOULD HAVE THOUGHT?

A number of machines we rely on today exist because of Thomas Edison's inventions and improvements. Edison invented the **phonograph** in 1879. It was the first machine that could record and play sound. In 1879, he made improvements to the telephone. He also created a **kinetoscope**. That was the first machine that could produce a moving image. That invention led to the machines that play your favorite movies in theaters.

Power to the People

In the beginning, all power stations were like Edison's. The current flowed in one direction. That was the way electricity was delivered to homes and buildings. Then Nikola Tesla (1856–1943) invented a **generator** that created a different kind of electricity.

Tesla's 1887 generator turned around the flow of electrons many times a second. It was called **alternating current (AC)** electricity. In many ways, AC outdid the older kind of electricity. It could travel long distances with much more power. Today, homes and other buildings are powered by AC electricity.

Imagine if Tesla could tell his story today . . .

Meet James Watt

James Watt (1736–1819) was a Scottish engineer. Inside every power plant is a generator that turns one kind of energy into electrical power. It was Watt's work that helped lead the way for this. He improved the steam engine in 1765. That eventually changed the way we produce electricity. Watt's steam engine used the pressure from steam to make electricity.

HOLD YOUR HORSES!

There was a battle between my backers and Thomas Edison.

Edison had invested a lot of money in his kind of power plants.

He tried to turn the public against the idea of AC electricity. Yet AC won out.

I didn't stop there.

After seeing a picture of Niagara Falls, I dreamed of finding a way to capture the energy of the falling water. I wanted to use that energy to create electricity.

In 1896, it happened! I helped to open the first **hydroelectric power plant** at Niagara Falls.

Not all of Tesla's ideas worked out—or at least they haven't yet. For example, he imagined that one day we might be able to pull electricity from lightning.

Does Electricity Flow through Every Material?

You Will Need:

2 strips of aluminum foil, 12 inches long by 1 inch wide

Tape

1.5-volt light bulb (from a flashlight)

D-cell battery

3 clothespins

Testing materials: For example, penny, paper clip, piece of wool, pencil, piece of fruit, leaf

1 Tape the end of one of the aluminum foil strips to the bottom end of the battery.

2 Wrap the end of the other foil strip around the bottom of a flashlight bulb. Clamp a clothespin over the foil to keep it in place.

3 Hold on to the clothespin. Place the bottom of the light bulb against the top end of the battery. Connect the free ends of the foil together. Use a clothespin to hold them together. That closes the circuit. The bulb should light up. Separate the foil pieces right after that so they do not have a chance to heat up.

4 Test different materials to see if electricity flows through them well. Use clothespins to attach the free ends of the foil strips to opposite sides of materials, such as a penny or a paper clip. If the bulb lights up, the material conducts electricity. That means electricity flows through it. The brighter the light, the better the object is at conducting electricity.

WHO WOULD HAVE THOUGHT?

Watt's steam engine design led to modern power stations. Today, roughly 86 percent of the world's electricity is still created by power plants with steam engines.

His invention helped start the Industrial Revolution. This was the period during the late 1800s and early 1900s when major improvements in machines changed life in a big way. Almost every part of your life is affected by the changes that happened during that time.

Timeline

500–600 BCE
Scientists in Ancient Greece produce static electricity by rubbing amber with wool and fur.

1600
William Gilbert becomes the first person to use the word *electric* when he publishes *De Magnete*, a book that included everything that was then known about electricity and magnetism.

1752
Benjamin Franklin proves that lightning is static electricity by flying a kite with a metal key attached to it in the middle of a thunderstorm.

1765
James Watt improves the steam engine, which will be used to make electricity.

1791
Luigi Galvani suggests that animal tissues create electricity after he observes a frog's muscles twitching while he dissects it with metal instruments.

1800
Alessandro Volta announces that he has invented the world's first battery, a pile of metal disks known as a voltaic pile.

1896

The Niagara Falls hydroelectric plant begins delivering alternating current electricity to homes using a generator based on Tesla's designs.

1887

Nikola Tesla invents a generator that creates electricity with an alternating current.

1882

Edison opens the Pearl Street Central Power Station—one of the first power plants to deliver electricity to homes and buildings in a large area.

1879

Thomas Edison offers his electric light bulb, which had a filament that burned for forty hours.

1831

Faraday produces the world's first dynamo, or generator, by spinning a copper plate around a magnet and creating an electric current.

1821

Michael Faraday shows how to produce mechanical energy from electrical energy, creating the first electric motor.

NEWS

Glossary

amber Fossilized fluid from trees.

alternating current (AC) Electricity in which the flow turns around many times in a second.

atom Smallest particle of any kind of matter.

bifocals Eyeglasses with divided lenses; the top helps people see far away; the bottom helps people see things that are close.

compass Instrument that uses a magnetized needle to show directions.

convert To change from one thing to another.

copper A reddish-brown metal.

current In electricity, the flow of electrons.

disk Tiny plate-shaped item.

dynamo Mechanical device that turns movement into electrical energy.

electromagnet Magnet using the flow of electrical current.

electrons Tiny electrically charged particles in an atom.

electrophorous Item that can store electric charge and deliver it later.

filament Fine metal wire in a light bulb.

generator Machine that makes electrical power.

International Space Station Space station being built by numerous countries, including the United States, for use by international scientists.

kinetoscope First machine to produce a moving image.

Leyden jar Special jar that stores static electricity.

lightning rod Rod placed on top of building to attract lightning.

magnetisim The property of one object's being able to attract another object.

mechanical energy The ability of something that is moving to do useful work.

particles Tiny units of matter.

phonograph Early machine that played sound.

solar panels Panels that take in heat from the Sun and turn it to energy.

static electricity Electric charge that is built up yet doesn't go anywhere.

terminal A point on the battery where current enters or leaves.

volt Unit measuring the strength or force of an electric current.

voltaic pile First battery, named for Alessandro Volta.

zinc A bluish-white metal.

Index